Planting schemes from

FRANCES LINCOLN

MONET'S GARDEN

VIVIAN RUSSELL

Brimming with creative inspiration, how-to projects and useful information to enrich your everyday life, Quarto Knows is a favourite destination for those pursuing their interests and passions. Visit our site and dig deeper with our books into your area of interest: Quarto Creates, Quarto Cooks, Quarto Homes, Quarto Lives, Quarto Drives, Quarto Explores, Quarto Gifts, or Quarto Kids.

Planting Schemes from Monet's Garden
Copyright © 2003 Quarto Publishing plc
Text and photographs copyright © 2003 Vivian Russell

First published in 2003 by Frances Lincoln,
an imprint of The Quarto Group,
The Old Brewery, 6 Blundell Street,
London N7 9BH, United Kingdom
T (0)20 7700 6700 F (0)20 7700 8066
www.QuartoKnows.com

Designed by Caroline Hillier

A catalogue record for this book is available from the British Library

ISBN 978-0-7112-1787-4

Printed and bound in China
20 19 18 17 16 15 14 13

HALF-TITLE Monet liked to create a feeling of intimacy in the garden by placing tall plants right at your feet. Here, verbascums, *Gladiolus* 'Merry' and *Coreopsis tinctoria* are planted flush with the path.

TITLE PAGE The 'jungle of beauty' that is Monet's flower garden.

Contents

Early in the spring of 1883, after yet another eviction notice, the forty-three-year-old Monet set off to find a house for himself, his two sons, his companion Alice Hoschedé and her six children. He would not return, he said, until he had found a house where they could stay put. He wanted to be near his beloved Seine, whose moods and mists he had so often painted, and he needed somewhere with reasonable schools for the older children.

He headed for the outskirts of Vernon, a town by the River Epte – a tributary of the Seine – some eighty kilometres north-west of Paris, and found what he was looking for in the outlying village of Giverny. The house was not hard to spot, having been painted sugar pink by a former owner to remind him of his sunny native Guadeloupe. It had been a cider farm, and its orchard of apples, in full blossom, presented a picture of irresistible charm. By a miracle, it was available to rent. Monet hoped that this move would be his last, and so it proved to be.

What he did not know was that he was at a crossroads. The first half, life before Giverny, was now over; the second half was about to begin. He lived for another forty-three years and during this time transformed the orchard into a flower garden of such startling originality that even now, more than a century later, it stands alone. The water garden he created across the road, loosely modelled on a Japanese stroll garden, would inspire the paintings that pushed art through the frontier of the twenty-first century.

The design and planting style of his flower garden was entirely of his own devising. It sprang from a love of wild flowers and commonly grown plants, which he massed together in long rectangular beds and square areas of orchard that formed a geometric grid. The blueprint for this layout can be traced to the Dutch tulip fields he went to paint in 1886: there tulips and hyacinths were planted in serried ranks to form bold and brilliant mosaic sheets of uniform colour across the flat polder. However, one observer read more prosaic origins into Monet's flower garden, comparing it to a glorified allotment, in which flowers replaced rows of carrots and beans.

When painting his landscapes, Monet was forever talking about capturing his 'effects'. These effects, which relied on atmospheric conditions and fleeting light, were by nature transitory, and often eluded him. He planted his garden for effects too, and these, though less elusive, were no less eagerly awaited.

Interestingly, Monet did very few paintings of his flower garden, content to leave it as a living canvas, complete with its palette of thirty-eight smaller 'paintbox beds' which sat, side by side, in parallel rows, like swatches of colour in a paintbox. These were his trial beds, where he would test new plants for colour, habit and vitality before integrating them into the main borders.

The few paintings of the flower garden that exist, together with surviving photographs, reveal that he created his effects by massing single species together in their various hues and then waiting for them to flower. In May it was the irises, in June, the pink and red peony border; in July the spotlight turned on the delphiniums. In one of his letters he mentions the campanula bed.

The Grande Allée became the focus of the garden in late summer and autumn. The borders on either side were identically planted with a row of pink and white Japanese anemones at the top, mauve asters in the middle and the famous orange nasturtiums at the bottom, scrambling to meet up in the middle of the path.

It was above all a colourist's garden, which Monet made according to his own taste and for his own pleasure. He liked clarity of colour but was not a colour snob. His likes and dislikes were not dictated by fashion, but driven by an instinctive horror of plants that looked unnatural (this was why he loathed variegated foliage, for instance). There was no distinction to be made in Monet's aesthetic between the colours he used in his paintings and the colours he used and juxtaposed in his garden. Orange, pink, red and yellow were all celebrated in appointed harmonies.

Exuberant planting contained within a formal design was one of the great themes of twentieth-century gardening. But more often than not, these 'jungles of beauty', as they were called, were edged with box hedges that, like double yellow lines, created a threshold you did not cross. Thus compartmentalized, the garden was kept at arm's length. One of the first things Monet did when he began gardening at Giverny was to remove the box that ran along both sides of the Grande Allée. He banked up the soil to make the plants seem even taller than they were, eventually replaced the overhanging spruces with rose-covered arches and laid trailing nasturtiums at your feet. The effect is like walking through a flowering tunnel. Similarly, tall plants usually grown at the back of a wide border were brought to the fore in a network of narrow paths and narrow borders so that, in late summer, walking along the paths is almost like walking through a corn maze.

After Monet's death in 1926 the garden inevitably declined, and many years were to elapse before the late Gerald van der Kemp, who also saved

Versailles, stepped in. He recognized its potential and its importance in France's cultural heritage, and obtained the necessary funds from America to rescue this rare horticultural treasure from oblivion. The restoration took three years, and when it opened to the public for the first time in 1980, Monet's garden had been resurrected, and to a certain extent reinvented. To meet the cost of maintaining a garden as labour-intensive and finely honed as the flower garden, high visitor numbers were essential, and compromises had to be made. Although the layout, plants and colour harmonies were faithfully preserved and recreated, the planting had to be adapted to provide interest for seven months of the year.

Over nearly a quarter of a century now, this reinvented garden has been acquiring a character of its own, and it has evolved into a work of art in its own right. Monet's garden has a timeless quality about it. It does not date, because it is not rooted in any style or convention that has grown stale with over-use. While the pendulum of fashion has swung this way and that, Monet's garden has stayed true to itself throughout. It may not be the garden you see in the paintings, but it is Monet's garden as it is now that people fall in love with.

So how does one go about capturing some of that Monet magic for oneself? The nuts and bolts of the colour and planting schemes as practised by the gardeners of Giverny today are outlined in this little book. But equally important to the magic of the garden is the psychology which underpins the planting. Monet's garden dazzles because it involves and envelops you. It manages to combine atmosphere, intimacy and accessibility with a sense of wonder at the profusion of its flowers. It is a tactile garden and, quite simply, it is a garden that you are happy to be in.

Into Spring with

Blossom and Bulbs

Flowering Fruit Trees

Daffodils and Crown Imperials

Pansies and Forget-me-nots

Tulips and Companions

The light frothy blossom of the crab apple *(Malus floribunda)*, carried high, and the strong clear pink of tulip 'Esther' compliment Monet's sugar-pink stucco house. Pale orange and yellow and white flowers are dotted about for a pointillist effect.

Spring steals gently into Giverny a whole month before the garden opens to the public. First in flower in early March is the purple aubrieta; then comes the soft pink blossom of Monet's crab apple outside the kitchen window, underplanted with a primrose-coloured wallflower (*Erysimum cheiri*). Elsewhere, the flowering cherries, plums and apple trees run the gamut of light and dark pink blossoms, their clouds of frothy pink carried high over the garden, echoing the warm pink stucco of the house façade.

Beneath the trees, the lawns are decorated with drifts of yellow trumpet daffodils and pale poet's or pheasant's eye narcissi with their warm orange-fringed centres; other narcissi planted in straight rows along borders give off a wonderful scent when you brush past them.

In April a blaze of tulips overtakes the soft harmonies – mauves, pinks, primroses and creams – of early spring. Lines of Dutch tulips in every hue are followed by Rembrandt tulips with mottled and marbled petals, making brilliant patches of colour. Yellow and orange crown imperials (*Fritillaria imperialis*) lend a stately air and mix dramatically with darker tulips.

Spring is when the bulbous and rhizomatous plants reign supreme. As well as narcissi, daffodils, tulips and fritillaries, eremurus and later irises each take their turn centre stage. None of these stars, though, would shine so clearly were it not for their supporting cast. The bright flowerheads of the larger bulbs float above blue forget-me-nots or jostle with massed pansies or wallflowers in many colours, all in a cottagey jumble.

Early spring finds the gardeners preoccupied with maintaining woody plants, particularly the roses and fruit trees. In February they tidy up summer-flowering roses, which were pruned hard in August, and hard-prune repeat-flowering (remontant) roses. Both kinds are tied in their shaping supports. When the pruning is finished in early March, the garden is treated with a copper-sulphate fungicide.

Other members of the gardening team work on the ceaseless task of keeping the beds planted for the coming season. They have set out spring-flowering biennials – pansies and wallflowers. These will be followed by waves of short-lived summer-flowering annuals and biennials as well as some perennials, all of which are sown in succession in the greenhouses depending on when they are planned to flower. They are planted out over a three-month period according to their hardiness. The earliest to emerge are *Leucanthemum* × *superbum*, Canterbury bells (*Campanula medium*) and foxgloves (*Digitalis purpurea*); next are honesty (*Lunaria rediviva*) and sweet rocket (*Hesperis matronalis*); the most fragile – varieties of bachelor's button – are not planted until June. The gardeners pot on seedlings in a light, poor soil mixed with perlite for good drainage; the meagre soil encourages development of strong roots as they scramble about looking for nutrients, which allows young plants to survive outside early in the season, after they have first been hardened off in a tunnel. A proportion of plants is always held back against the havoc of freak weather.

Just before the garden opens some final manicuring touches are applied. In the ribbons of aubrieta lining the paths, any plants suffocated by last season's annuals spilling over them or damaged by winter wet and cold are replaced so that there are no gaps. Like the edges of the lawns, the aubrieta is trimmed with military precision: a piece of string is stretched along the path and the plants are cut flush with it. Any other rockery or edging plants that need attention are tidied, and the garden is ready to open its gates.

The blossom of cherries and crab apples dominates the garden in April. Here, the electric-pink blossom of one of the crab apples presents a perfect foil to the pale pink façade of the house. The branches are pruned in the Japanese style to encourage a spreading, almost horizontal growth.

LEFT and ABOVE Cordon-trained apple trees frame an oasis of grass. In early spring the lawns blaze with daffodils and narcissi, which in turn will fade to leave a simple grassy setting. This will be screened off later in the summer by rows of tall hollyhocks – their distinctive scalloped leaves are seen here.

OVERLEAF Pale yellow *Erysimum cheiri* beneath Monet's original crab apple.

LEFT A fresh new tapestry of flowers unrolls with narcissi, arabis, the first of the purple aubrieta and a few early pink tulips.

ABOVE Crown imperials combine with swathes of daffodils, narcissi and tulips to make up the garden's bold spring palette.

Purple and wine-red pansies mingle with pale blue forget-me-nots in an Impressionist colour combination.

LEFT In a vibrant border different tulips, including orange Lily-flowered 'Ballerina', mingle with wallflowers, pansies and other spring flowers.

BELOW Tulip 'Ballerina' with wallflowers.

Tulips, wallflowers and aubrieta unfurl in a multicoloured wave, as spring gets under way in the Grande Allée. In Monet's time the limestone hills in the background, now gone to rough grass and woodland, were covered with a mosaic of cultivated crops.

LEFT Red and yellow was one of Monet's favourite colour schemes, and he explored it in his paintings long before he started gardening. Here it is worked in the ultra-bold colours of Triumph tulips – red 'Paul Richter' and yellow 'Mamasa' – floating above yellow and orange wallflowers.

ABOVE Anomalies sometimes occur. Here some 'Blue Parrot' tulips have arrived unexpectedly in the midst of a planting of red-slashed yellow 'Apeldoorn's Elite' and red Lily-flowered 'Marjolein', surrounded by wallflower 'Ruby Gem' and pansy 'Erfurt'.

ABOVE Lily-flowered tulip 'West Point' grows with *Erysimum cheiri* 'Mascott' in a sea of yellow, while RIGHT wallflower 'Fire King' and tulip 'Prinses Irene' make '*un coin orange*', nuanced from light to dark, and OVERLEAF island beds glow with tulips including 'Blue Parrot', 'Burgundy' and 'Bleu Aimable', wallflower 'Ruby Gem' and blue *Cynoglossum nervosum*.

Lily-flowered tulip
'White Triumphator'
mingles with white
forget-me-nots to create
a vision of green and
white. In the foreground,
to the right, alliums are
in bud.

LEFT White daisy-like *Leucanthemum maximum* flowers with striped tulip 'Sorbet', against a background of white and mauve forget-me-nots and brown-faced cream pansies.

ABOVE The tulips 'Angélique', 'Preludium', 'Esther' and 'Aristocrat', together with pink and yellow wallflowers and red and mauve pansies, are the basic ingredients of a pink and red border. The ever-present aubrieta edges the paths.

LEFT Purple *Fritillaria persica* 'Adiyaman' jostles with mauve pansies, red wallflowers and pink and green tulip 'Groenland'.

ABOVE Purple tulip 'Negrita' rises up from a bed of white violas.

Spring into Summer
A Shifting Kaleidoscope

Irises

Peonies

Daisies and Sweet Rocket

Poppies

Roses

In a glorious combination that evokes a summer meadow, Shasta daisies (*Leucanthemum × superbum*) and sweet rocket (*Hesperis matronalis* var. *albiflora*) are peppered with purple irises and orange wallflowers.

Giverny is sublime during May and June. As the red and yellow spring bulbs finish, the garden becomes a vision of blues and mauves. The stars of the season are the irises, which Monet grew in every imaginable variant of colour and form, and the aubrieta-edged beds of tall irises in blues, violets, purples and white are the pride of the garden.

The irises – well suited to the alkaline soil of Giverny – flower happily for weeks, with early and late cultivars to prolong the show. Sweet rocket (*Hesperis matronalis*) and masses of white *Leucanthemum* × *superbum* provide a contrast to the blues and mauves, while the fast-growing annual *Phacelia tanacetifolia* gives an effective blue transition as the biennials go over and the annuals begin.

As spring looks forward to summer, the garden moves from purple, blue and white to pink, white and purple. The stunning pink foxtail lily, eremurus, with enormous spikes of pink and of cream, gives height to the Grande Allée. Starry pink and white garlands of *Clematis montana* clamber over specially built frames, flourishing as they did in Monet's time.

Then the kaleidoscope turns once again. June marches in with a flamboyance of reds and rosy pinks, in the form of lush peonies, poppies like the scarlet field poppy (*Papaver rhoeas*) as well as many varieties of opium poppy (*Papaver somniferum*) with flowers in every nuance from slate-grey to vermilion red. Above all there are the roses, blowzy and exuberant, the hallmark of the June garden. Monet had a special penchant for roses overhead and in the vertical plane: as well as the roses growing on metal arches over the Grande Allée, standard roses in the borders form a permanent framework to an ever-changing planting beneath.

When the spring-flowering bulbs have finished they are lifted, except for the narcissi, which are left until the foliage is completely rotted, allowing them to multiply prodigiously. To take the bulbs' place, and to fill gaps left by fading perennials, hardy and half-hardy annuals raised in the greenhouse, such as snapdragons and the many varieties of tobacco, are planted out. Hardy annuals such as poppies that do not tolerate being transplanted are broadcast-sown in spaces in the borders. As summer-flowering bulbs, such as lilies and gladioli, go into the ground, the spring-flowering biennials are removed. The floral relay race for plants to succeed and overlap each other over several months requires meticulous planning and perfect synchronization; the gardeners rely on a policy of 'safety in numbers' and staggered sowings to ensure that there are no gaps.

Once the annuals are in, shaping and controlling growth becomes the gardeners' main concern. Young plants are pinched out to encourage bushiness and sturdy growth. Some need staking or the support of a stronger neighbour; peony supports are installed by May. The various climbers – clematis, roses, honeysuckle – all need training and tying in.

Every day the gardeners weed and pull out plants that have finished flowering or deadhead them, depending on the merits of their foliage – the discreet foliage of sweet rocket, for instance, is left, to act as a host for later annuals to grow through. Some perennials, such as cranesbill geranium 'Johnson's Blue', whose foliage tends to become leggy and sprawling, are cut right back after flowering, allowing room for annuals such as cosmos and cleome to be planted around them. The annuals grow up among the fresh green herbage of the shorn perennials, keeping the beds well furnished with flowers and interesting foliage.

The pale yellow centres
of pink Iceland poppies
echo the primrose colour
of *Erysimum cheiri*.

TOP *Iris pallida* and ABOVE *I.* 'Dark Triumph'.

LEFT Irises including variegated 'Joseph's Coat', purple 'Dark Triumph' and a yellow Dutch iris make a bold contrast.

ABOVE White 'Henry Shaw' irises break up the parade of purples in the iris beds.

RIGHT Irises grow under the trees in the orchard, just as they did in Monet's day.

OVERLEAF Nascent 'Ali Baba' oriental poppies are about to take their turn and flashes of 'Fire King' wallflowers glow among the irises.

ABOVE and RIGHT Peonies and sweet rocket nestle together as Giverny turns from blue and mauve to red and pink. *Paeonia lactiflora* cultivars relish the sunny site and limy soil, contributing pink profusion to the summer display.

This border running parallel to the Grande Allée is the only one in the garden which is predominantly white. The planting consists of alternating white daisies and sweet rocket (*Leucanthemum × superbum* and *Hesperis matronalis* var. *albiflora*) interspersed randomly with dashes of red provided by *Papaver orientale*. It makes a good transition bed, drawing the eye away from the adjacent border where the biennials are just fading.

LEFT Poppies of every hue have always been encouraged at Giverny. They are now so invasive that they need some thinning, but for the most part they are allowed to self-seed and grow where they fall.

RIGHT ABOVE *Papaver somniferum.*

RIGHT BELOW Palest pink *P. orientale* 'Karine' with a white *P. orientale* cultivar.

BELOW The red common or field poppy (*Papaver rhoeas*) that almost became Monet's trademark.

RIGHT Monet enjoyed mixing wild flowers with exotic. Here, the self-seeding common poppy grows through *Lilium* 'Massa'.

A profusion of pink, red and purple roses and poppies smothers the outlines of the Grande Allée.

LEFT In early summer, before the Grande Allée really comes into its own, pink and red roses, including 'Paul's Scarlet Climber', trained over the arches, distract the eye from the borders. So too do the two delft jardinières at the end of the vista. These are similar to Monet's original pots, which feature in several of his pre-Giverny paintings of his gardens in Argenteuil and Vétheuil.

BELOW Rose 'Paul's Scarlet Climber'.

LEFT Roses growing overhead and in the vertical plane are a feature of the garden at Giverny. Here the pink *Rosa* 'Clair Matin' flowers profusely on a pergola with *R*. 'Crimson Shower' and *R*. 'Cramoisi Supérieur' alongside.

RIGHT 'Pillar' roses – tall-growing cultivars meant to be grown on supports in upright, columnar shapes – were developed at the end of the nineteenth century, just when Monet was planting the garden. With his penchant for climbing roses, they must have suited him perfectly. This method of training them by wrapping their main stems around a triangular support is characteristic of Giverny.

LEFT and BELOW This 'Centenaire de Lourdes' rose has been trained into a 'cloche' (bell) or 'champignon' (mushroom) shape, following a framework or 'armature'.

High Summer

Flowery Profusion

Purple Tones

Yellow Paintbox

Cosmos and Cleomes

Hollyhocks

Summer Glory

The gardeners often add white to set off an otherwise monochromatic planting. Here white *Nicotiana sylvestris* and crown daisies (*Xanthophthalmum coronarium*) are planted among yellow and orange corn marigolds (*Xanthophthalmum segetum*), *Cosmos sulphureus* and *Rudbeckia hirta*.

The summer spectacle is a sumptuous one. Today's visitors still find the plants that Monet grew, no longer planted in masses of one variety as he had them but mingled everywhere in mixed border style, so as to ensure that the display hums a steady flowery tune throughout the summer months. By July, the hollyhocks, delphiniums and cleomes all rise tall, adding their glory to the summer garden, as do *Salvia guaranitica*, *Nicotiana sylvestris* and *Lythrum salicaria*. The nasturtiums that figure prominently in the later summer and autumn garden are growing vigorously. Roses such as 'The Queen Elizabeth' and the modern Hybrid Teas take over from the earlier flowerers and provide flowers well into August.

The gardeners are kept busy looking after the taller-growing plants whose performance does not get under way until towards the end of summer. By the end of June the asters and dahlias need staking with the gardener Gilbert Vahé's famous green-painted *fers à béton*. The giants such as hollyhocks, sunflowers and anchusa also need the strong support of the *fers à béton*. Once these plants become top-heavy, their stems are impossible to straighten, and they fall over and crack in the middle. Very slender bamboos with supple wire or thin string are used to support finer plants such as solidago and *Coreopsis tinctoria*. Every third stem is staked and supports the two neighbouring plants as well. The much-used bachelor's button is too spindly to stake unobtrusively, so the gardeners find for it hosts such as hollyhocks and phlox.

The nasturtiums in the borders alongside the Grande Allée need careful training now, to create the spectacular effect so special to Giverny. When their stems reach some 35–50 centimetres (15–20 inches) long, the gardeners start guiding them towards the middle of the path. Once they reach 90 centimetres (36 inches), the leaves and growing tips are cut back to reveal the flowers and put a break on their growth.

The task of dividing and replanting the bearded irises is very time-consuming. Ideally it is done every two years, in July and August, but sometimes the gap has to be extended to four years. When they are dug up, any weak or diseased plants are thrown out and the best ones are selected for replanting. The healthy portions of rhizome are cut; this year's and last year's growth is kept and the older, congested material is discarded. The roots are trimmed to 5–10 centimetres (2–4 inches) and the leaves are neatened. The tallest (and oldest) leaves are cut halfway down in a point, leaving the newest leaves intact in the middle. The trimming minimizes water loss, prevents the newly planted rhizomes from being rocked by the wind and looks more '*ésthetique*'. The rhizomes are replanted in two neat rows following wires (which are later removed) running the length of the beds. It is important to keep them weeded; the gardeners put granules of selective weed-killer on the surface of the soil to suppress the germination of weed seedlings.

Hollyhocks have always grown well in Giverny. However, a careful watch must be mounted to prevent the rust to which these plants are notoriously susceptible. They are sprayed once a week in spring, as soon as their leaves are out, but by June the gardeners are too busy to find time to continue this treatment. They have to trust that the early preventive spraying has done the trick. All they can do now is keep an eye on them, and if either rust or red spider mite is spotted, the affected leaves are removed and destroyed.

LEFT Monet made a special point of collecting
blue flowers. In this monochromatic blue
border the sprawling blue potato bush, *Solanum
rantonnetii* (close-up ABOVE), is counterpointed
by a spear-like deep blue delphinium,
discreetly staked by a green-painted *fer à béton*.
A white *Cleome hassleriana* sets off the blues.

LEFT Surrounding five large yellow *Solidago canadensis* a pointilliste-style planting in oranges and yellows includes: *Tagetes erecta* F1 hybrids 'Diamond Jubilee', Golden Jubilee', 'Sovereign' and 'Doubloon'; *Rudbeckia hirta* 'Marmalade' (close-up BELOW); hollyhocks; *Coreopsis tinctoria* 'Elegant'; *Cosmos sulphureus*; *Zinnia mexicana* 'Old Mexico'; *Asclepias curassavica*; and *Gladiolus* 'Merry'. The bed is edged with *Chrysanthemum segetum*, *Oenothera fruticosa* 'Youngii', *Sanvitalia procumbens* and English lavender.

LEFT Tall verbascums, *Gladiolus* 'Merry' and *Coreopsis tinctoria* growing at the edge of the path.

ABOVE *Rudbeckia fulgida* var. *sullivantii* 'Goldsturm' and *Gladiolus* 'Merry' in another pink and yellow combination flecked with white. Monet loved bicoloured flowers, of which this gladiolus is a particularly lovely example.

In a midsummer planting in a west-facing border, the bold chocolate-purple foliage of *Amaranthus tricolor* and the white flowers of tobacco plant *Nicotiana sylvestris* are surrounded by a cottagey jumble of yellow and orange. The planting is dominated by mahogany-centred *Rudbeckia hirta* Mon Plaisir Group and *R. fulgida* – brilliant yellow with black centres. *Chrysanthemum segetum*, *Cosmos sulphureus* 'Diablo' and *Lysimachia punctata* add smaller splashes of yellow and orange, while *Salvia farinacea* 'Victoria' provides a blue accent. Monet deliberately planted orange, red and yellow flower borders on the west side of the garden to catch the long golden rays of the setting sun and heighten the glow.

TOP A white cleome with electric-pink
Cleome hassleriana behind.

ABOVE *Cleome hassleriana.*

RIGHT *Solanum rantonnetii, Cosmos bipinnatus*
'White Sensation' and *C.b.* 'Gloria',
veronica, *Ageratum houstonianum* 'Top Blue'

ABOVE Hollyhocks were great favourites of Monet, and were among the first flowers to be planted at Giverny. They seed themselves freely, in all colours, and whether they are pulled out or left depends on the goodwill of the gardeners. Beneath the hollyhock in the picture RIGHT is a *Phlox drummondii*, and on the other side of the path is *Anthemis tinctoria* 'Kelwayi'.

RIGHT Deep pink hollyhocks tower over phlox
in a paler pink.

BELOW A white hollyhock is visited by a bee.

The combination of mallow (*Malva sylvestris* cv), self-seeding poppies (*Papaver somniferum*) and pale pink roses in one of the paintbox beds presents a picture of old-fashioned cottage garden charm.

The North American prairie plant *Gaura lindheimeri* is airy, elegant and graceful. The individual flowers may be short-lived, but they are produced from late spring to early autumn.

LEFT *Nicotiana* 'Nicki Red', the pink *Rosa* 'Hermosa', *Gladiolus* 'Elvira' about to open, *Antirrhinum majus* 'Sweet Crimson', *Lilium* 'Côte d'Azur' and a touch of the silver *Tanacetum ptarmiciflorum*.

BELOW *Nicotiana* 'Domino Purple' and *Zinnia* 'Lavender Dream' in a duet of purple and mauve.

LEFT In late July, annual sunflowers are already rising tall among nicotianas, cleomes and cosmos, while rudbeckias, perennial helianthus and other yellow annuals and perennials which will camouflage the house are beginning their ascent.

BELOW The orange nasturtiums and pink cosmos in the Grande Allée repeat the pink and orange theme that brings a late summer glow to the flower garden.

Extending Colour

into Autumn

Asters and Sunflowers

Roses and Salvias

Cosmos

Long-lasting Cleomes

Dahlias

Late Purples

The light pinks of *Cosmos bipinnatus* 'Candy Stripe' and *C.b.* 'Versailles Red' are enhanced by the almost chocolate-coloured dahlia 'Arabian Night'.

Autumn at Giverny is the most atmospheric and magical of seasons. Like so many smiling faces, a few enormous sunflowers and the many yellow blooms of the lanky *Helianthus × multiflorus* are the first to peep through. Next come the Cactus dahlias which reign over the borders. Dahlias were Monet's first love, and Giverny has a huge range. Clouds of asters offset the heaviness of the dahlias and sunflowers. The garden glows in a mantle of red, pink, purple and gold, enhanced by reddening, yellowing foliage everywhere. Marigolds, heleniums, heliopsis, rudbeckias and many varieties of helianthus carry the autumnal torch for the golds and yellows. The cleomes gradually turn into decorative spiky seedheads, their pink and white theme picked up now by the prolific flowers of pink and white cosmos.

The Grande Allée is at its peak, glowing in purple and yellow. It is flanked on each side by the dark red *Dahlia* 'Jet' and mauve asters, and the *pièce de résistance* is the famous carpet of trailing nasturtiums, now all blazing. By mid-September, only a narrow sinuous path is visible between the sea of undulating leaves, brilliantly translucent in the sun and making waves of frothy acid-green on which float orange flowers.

The climbers that clothe the garden's verticals become red, orange and yellow, making a fiery background to the flowers in the garden. The leaves of the Virginia creeper (*Parthenocissus quinquefolia*) that covers part of the house take on their distinctive deep red autumnal colouring and make a vibrant impact against the pink stucco of the walls.

Autumnal golds and oranges do not mean the end of the blues, mauves, pinks and whites in the garden. Dominating the blue borders are perennial blue asters – *Aster novae-angliae* – and the white *A. laevis*, all flowering with the same vigour as in Monet's time. The rich mauve-blue flowers of *Solanum rantonnetii*, the mallows and *Salvia* 'Indigo', among others, provide a harmonious backdrop for the blue and white asters.

The painstaking and time-consuming attention the gardeners have paid to the *tuteurage* – the neat tying up and staking – now fulfils its purpose and keeps the garden on its feet until the end of October. Storms and winds can do their worst, but the dahlias and sunflowers safely anchored to their metal stakes stay upright and unassailable until vanquished by frost. Two gardeners are charged with the job of going around the garden double-checking the labelling of the countless varieties of dahlia and evaluating their performance.

By mid-September the gardeners no longer have to cut back the annuals or perennials to prevent them from spilling over on to neighbouring plants. Instead they spend the mornings deadheading and weeding, and keeping the garden clear of fallen leaves. All through September and October, biennials are gradually planted out from greenhouse to nursery fields, as the gardeners begin the seasonal cycle again with next year's plantings.

When the garden closes at the end of October, it is cleared and tidied. The dahlias are dug up and laid out in the garage to dry for eight to ten days before being stored in the cellar on a layer of peat. Annuals and biennials are thrown away. The foliage of larger perennials such as asters, solanum, helianthus and peonies is cut down. Perennials are never allowed to grow too large, but are kept the same desired size. Each plant is dug up, inspected, its roots and top trimmed; then it is given a good shaking and replanted. The soil is dug over and cow manure is incorporated, along with a slow-acting, general-purpose fertilizer. Bulbs are planted for the following year.

LEFT A swathe of nasturtiums carpets the path between banks of bright yellow *Helianthus × laetiflorus*, dark red *Dahlia* 'Jet' and mauve asters. The nasturtium seeds are planted in spring, directly into the soil on either side of the path. When they begin to grow they are encouraged to creep towards one another and towards the light in the middle of the path.

OVERLEAF A bed filled with the typical golds, yellows and purples of the autumn garden. Here are helianthus, asters, *Cosmos bipinnatus* 'Versailles Red' and *C.b.* 'White Sensation', the self-seeding *Impatiens valfourii*, the Cactus dahlia 'Czardas' and the ubiquitous dahlia 'Jet'. In the background is a standard 'Palissade Rose'.

BELOW The half-hardy Mexican sunflower *Tithonia rotundifolia* 'Torch' lights up the border on the dullest day.

RIGHT Marigolds (*Tagetes erecta* cv), *Tithonia rotundifolia* 'Torch', *Helianthus annuus* cv and asters recreate the combination of yellow, orange and mauve that Monet loved.

LEFT Even in November this combination of rose 'Phyllis Bide', *Salvia involucrata* 'Bethellii' and *Cosmos bipinnatus* makes a festive sight. The roses have to be carefully pruned and tied in, so as to appear to be growing naturally yet not dwarf or shade their neighbours.

ABOVE A pink and yellow border. Underpinned by *Cosmos bipinnatus* 'Versailles Red' and yellow marigolds, the long branching stems and racemes of *Salvia involucrata* 'Bethellii' and tall yellow helianthus carry pink and yellow high into the sky for a wild garden effect.

LEFT ABOVE *Cosmos bipinnatus* 'Picotee'.

LEFT BELOW *C.b.* 'Sensation'.

RIGHT *C.b.* 'Versailles Red' and *C.b.* 'Picotee'.

These three cosmos cultivars are massed together in true Monet style. Walking down the path between the cosmos borders is like wading through a sea of different pinks.

BELOW As prized for their luminous colour as for their spiky seedheads, cleomes add an exotic touch to the late summer garden. Monet planted wide swathes of *Cleome hassleriana*.

RIGHT A golden spreading *Albizia julibrissin* hovers protectively over a mixed bed that includes, as well as cleomes, *Zinnia* 'Purple Prince', the prolific *Helianthus* × *laetiflorus*, *Cosmos bipinnatus* and verbascums.

ABOVE A yellow Semi-cactus dahlia.

RIGHT The pale pink façade of the
house rises from a sea of deep pink
cosmos and velvety red dahlias.

LEFT ABOVE Collerette dahlia 'Libretto'.

LEFT BELOW A red Cactus dahlia.

BELOW The dark red dahlia 'Arabian Night'.

RIGHT ABOVE Orchid-flowering dahlia 'Jescot Julie'.

RIGHT BELOW Cactus dahlia 'Aumonier Chandelon'.

BELOW Cactus dahlia 'Jolie Normande'.

LEFT ABOVE Cactus dahlia 'Hayley Jayne'.

LEFT CENTRE Medium Decorative dahlia 'Lilac Time'.

LEFT BELOW Giant Decorative dahlia 'Emory Paul'.

RIGHT Pink cosmos alternates with the bicolored pink and orange Cactus dahlia 'Decorose' the whole length of this bed.

Heliotropium arborescens (syn. *H. peruvianum*) adds scent to the autumn garden.

The autumn-flowering *Crocus sativus*, with prominent orange stigmas which are dried to produce saffron, grows on the large east lawn.

The Water Garden

Winter into Spring

Spring Waterside Planting

Early Summer Flowers

Willows, Bamboos and Water Lilies

Summer Waterside Annuals

Autumn Colours

Even on a sombre day, too late for water lily flowers and too early for autumn colour, the mirrored surface of the pond is alive with subtle nuances of green.

The water garden is perhaps at its loveliest and most luminous in early spring, when the buds are breaking and the light shining through unclothed branches and reflecting off the water adds sparkle to the many hues of yellow and green, underplanted here and there with clumps of the poet's narcissi and daffodils. Elsewhere, there are small treasures – the snakeshead fritillary, *Anemone blanda*, then tulips and a carpet of white-flowering sweetly scented woodruff (*Galium odoratum*) under the weeping willow that Monet planted himself.

While the garden is shut the gardeners drain the pond, then weed and remove the algae – a laborious job, all done by hand. They divide the water lilies, clean them up, and replant them, replacing any that have been damaged by muskrats over the winter from a reserve kept in a cement pool near the greenhouse. The pond is then refilled.

The delicacy of early spring is replaced in late April by a sturdier show – mature leaves, showy azaleas (*Rhododendron luteum* and *R.* 'Persil'), purple acers and *Viburnum opulus* – all underplanted with pansies and wallflowers.

From June on, the water garden, shaded by poplars and willows and framed by tall aspens, is covered with flowers of many colours. The Japanese bridge so familiar from Monet's paintings is covered with a marvellous decoration of the mauve *Wisteria floribunda* 'Multijuga' and *W. sinensis*, followed by the white *W. floribunda* 'Alba' and *W. sinensis* 'Alba'. In August, once they have all flowered, the wisterias are pruned to remove the bean-like seed pods and any untidy trailing shoots, as well as to encourage ripening of the flowering spurs. Carrying on the Japanese theme are other exotic plants such as bamboos and tree peonies. The peonies were planted by Monet to stand out as oriental 'accents'. Otherwise, the ornamental shrubs and trees with which the area is predominantly planted are grown not so much for their individual qualities as to make a setting for the pond.

On this mirror-like expanse of water, which appears reflective in one light and translucent in another, float Monet's last love, his water lilies. His concern for keeping the surface of the water clear was renowned: once the water lilies had become established, the gardeners had to keep their leaves trimmed so that they formed discrete floating rafts, rather than a continuous carpet. But while in Monet's time the gardeners had to struggle to curb the water lilies' rampant growth, today the lilies are lucky to survive the depredations of the muskrats that plague them.

Elsewhere in the water garden, acid-loving rhododendrons, kalmias, hollies and ferns increase steadily and slowly, helped by ample additions of acidic soil and peat. The gardeners use a special water-permeable wrapping for the roots of new calcifuge plants. This allows moisture in but keeps the calcareous elements out.

In autumn, the large trees and shrubs that have encircled the pond like discreet green wallpaper come into their own as their colours turn. A panorama of dark reds, rusts and oranges is reflected in the water. Now there is less need for constant trimming back to check plants' invasiveness, but the gardeners have to rake leaves from the water's surface to preserve its mirror-like appearance.

The water lilies are in groups of three, planted in a basket with handles for ease of movement. A post driven into the pond bed and just showing above the surface marks the position of each. The lilies are tended from a boat. After the garden closes, they are cut down with a scythe; stems, leaves and faded flowers are gathered up, together with any algae floating on the surface.

Snowdrops garnish the winter garden. Willows specially planted along the banks of the stream provide excellent garden stakes.

The wispy branches of
Monet's original weeping
willow hang like a
curtain around a carpet
of sweet woodruff
(*Galium odoratum*),
brightened by a clump
of red tulips.

ABOVE Monet's famous Japanese bridge looks skeletal against the colourless sky of early spring. However, the giant round leaves of petasites add an air of solidity to the scene.

RIGHT *Acer palmatum* 'Ornatum' and azalea 'Cecile' are rich and darkly dramatic, attracting attention in the spring months before the water lilies break through the surface of the water.

ABOVE The view from the path towards the Japanese bridge, in early summer.

RIGHT The long white racemes of *Wisteria sinensis* 'Alba' — Monet's original wisteria — clothe the bridge, creating a symphony in white and green.

RIGHT In May it is still too early for the water lilies
– though their stems have grown to the surface – but
meanwhile along the banks of the water garden the
large-flowered, primrose-coloured shrub rose 'Nevada'
and a clump of *Delphinium* Guinevere Group are in
flower.

BELOW Lavender-blue Dutch irises mingle with yellow
Iris pseudacorus at the edge of the pond.

ABOVE A tree peony (*Paeonia × lemoinei*) glows amidst dark mahonia foliage.

RIGHT At the edge of the water garden the sword-like foliage of *Iris sibirica*, with *Cotinus coggygria* and red and yellow *Aquilegia* 'Koralle', make a spare, rather oriental combination.

OVERLEAF In late spring Excelsior foxgloves, their trumpets flecked with black, red, pink and cream, combine opulently with a crimson rhododendron.

The western part of the pond, seen here during a sudden summer storm with rain pelting down on it, is like an overgrown jungle of green. It is punctuated by oriental accents planted by Monet himself, including the massive thicket of bamboos to the left and the wisteria and the species irises along the banks.

LEFT and BELOW The lime-green curtain of weeping willow makes a marvellous foil for cloud-like rafts of water lilies.

RIGHT Willow, bamboo and Japanese bridge come together in the water garden to create a secret, mysterious private world, surrounding the rafts of water lilies BELOW.

OVERLEAF The blue-green water alive with reflections, the delicate floating blooms of the water lily, their bold, distinctive rafts of leaves and the delicate curtain of weeping willow are the quintessential elements of the water garden, whose endlessly changing moods Monet strove to portray in his paintings.

LEFT and BELOW On the surface of the pond, water-lily pads float in the rafts that were described by Proust as floating flowerbeds. Monet deliberately grew them in discrete shapes rather than as a continuous spread, so as to keep clear the calm, unfathomable pond surface.

In Monet's time the pond was edged almost all the way round with different kinds of irises, among them the *Iris pseudacorus* pictured here. The banks were laid with grass and dotted with shrubs, principally tree peonies. The present gardeners have planted African marigolds (*Tagetes erecta*), corn marigolds (*Xanthophthalmum segetum*), *Asclepias tuberosa* and *Nicotiana* 'Lime Green' to make the water garden more floriferous for visitors and to prevent keen photographers from falling in the pond.

The bridge, inspired by
the Japanese woodblock
prints that decorated
Monet's house, started
life without the overhead
trellis. Added ten years
later and clothed with
wisteria, it provided yet
another layer of
reflection to the pond.
Monet painted it over
and over again during his
last years, continually
distilling it into its
essential elements until
he was left with just the
arch of the bridge and a
furore of greens.

Monet's pond in autumn turns to molten gold, set alight by the fiery foliage of a group of sweet gum trees (*Liquidambar styraciflua*). Late in his life this became a favourite motif, which he painted after his water lilies had ceased flowering.

In early autumn the water
garden shimmers in the
sunshine like an oriental
stage set. The wisteria
frames the view of the
weeping willow, which,
like a gold curtain, draws
the season to a close.

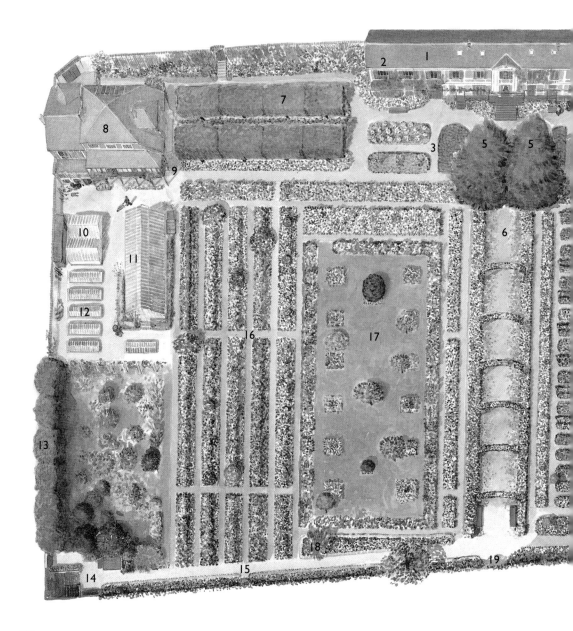

The Flower Garden

1 Monet's house
2 Monet's bedroom (above the first studio)
3 Island beds
4 Monet's original crab apple tree
5 Twin yews
6 Grande Allée with rose arches
7 Pleached limes, mostly original
8 Monet's second studio
9 Dovecote
10 New small greenhouses
11 New large greenhouse
12 Cold frames
13 Hedge of horse chestnut
14 Entrance to underground passage leading to the water garden
15 Boundary wall planted with pyracantha and climbing roses
16 15 monochromatic and polychromatic flower beds
17 Lawn with roses, fruit trees and square flower beds
18 Tamarisk tree
19 Former main gate
20 38 paintbox beds ('*les tombes*'), 7 pairs with clematis frames above
21 Monochromatic perennial flower beds
22 Espaliered apple trees
23 House formerly lived in by Monet's head gardener
24 Third studio, where the water lily panels were painted
25 Chicken and turkey yard

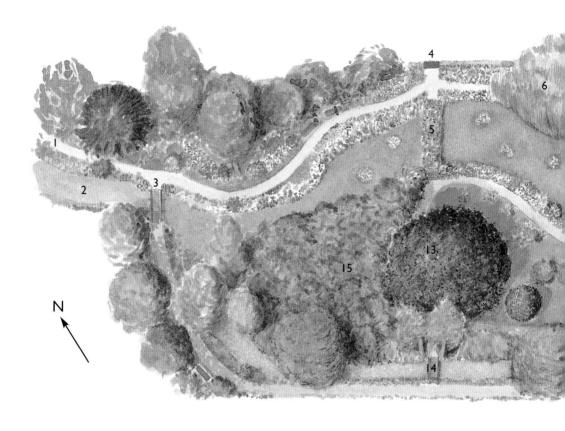

The Water Garden

1 Entrance to underground passage leading from the flower garden
2 River Ru, diverted by Monet to create the pond
3 Bridge
4 Former main gate on the axis of the Grande Allee, now used by the gardeners
5 The wisteria-covered Japanese bridge
6 Monet's original weeping willow
7 The pond with water lilies

8 Original wisteria, now supported on trellis
9 Bridge over old sluice gate
10 Bridge
11 Rose arches
12 Bridge
13 Copper beech, the site of Monet's tree peonies
14 Bridge
15 Bamboo thicket, planted by Monet

Index

Publishers' Acknowledgments

Design by Caroline Hillier

Editors Alison Freegard and Anne Askwith

Horticultural consultant Tony Lord

Production Kim Oliver

Index by Serena Dilnot

Plan illustrations by Joanna Logan